Contents

KU-862-931

Early life

Henry Ford was born on 30 July 1863, in Dearborn, Michigan, USA. His father was a farmer. His mother died in 1876, when Henry was only thirteen.

Henry went to Dearborn village school as a boy. He helped on the family farm. When he was sixteen he went to work as an **engineer** in nearby Detroit.

Steam engines

Henry moved back to Dearborn aged nineteen. He helped his father run the farm. He also hired out and ran a **steam engine** on neighbouring farms.

Someone from a steam engine company saw Henry at work. They gave him a job travelling around showing people how steam engines worked. They hoped this would make people buy one.

The Edison Illuminating Company

In 1888 Henry married Clara Bryant. Three years later he took a job at the Edison **Illuminating** Company, repairing **steam engines**.

Henry was so good at his job that by 1893 he was chief **engineer**. In the same year he and Clara had their only child, a son called Edsel.

Ford's first car

Henry and some other **engineers** began work on a **carriage** driven by an **engine**. At the time, carriages were pulled by horses. In 1896 this early car, the Quadricycle, was ready.

Henry tried to drive the machine out of its shed. But it was too wide! He and the other workers had to pull a wall down to get it out.

The Ford Motor Company

In 1903 Henry opened a motor car **factory**. By 1908 he was making the Ford Model T. He used **mass produced** parts. It was cheap and very **popular**.

By 1913 Henry's factory was using
assembly lines. Each worker on a line
did one small job on a piece of the car.
It was quicker and cheaper.

Later life

Henry bought a newspaper, the *Dearborn Independent.* He also set up a museum in Dearborn. In 1937 Orville Wright visited the museum. He was one of the inventors of the aeroplane.

Henry set up the first airport to carry air mail and use **radio** to guide aeroplanes. He also invented the Tri-Motor aeroplane. Henry died on 7 April 1947, aged 83.

Photographs

There are many ways we can find out about Henry Ford and his life. Photos show us what he and his family looked like.

Photos also show us what Henry's **factories** looked like. This photo shows us what **assembly lines** were like.

Written clues

The *Dearborn Independent* is the newspaper that Henry owned. It is full of articles that tell us what he thought about things. This paper is from 6 August 1921.

The Ford International Weekly

THE DEARBORN INDEPENDENT

By the Year $1.50   Dearborn, Michigan, August 6, 1921   Single Copy Ten Cents

COMPANION OF HER HOLIDAYS

Anticipations of a joyous, carefree vacation are abundantly realized when a Ford closed car provides easy access to town or country.

The attractive upholstery and all-weather equipment of the Fordor Sedan suggest comfort and protection on long trips, while the simple foot-pedal control assures ease of operation in crowded city traffic.

An increasing number of women who prefer to drive their own cars, are selecting the Ford Fordor Sedan for their personal use, knowing it to be an outstanding value as well as a possession in which they can take pride.

| TUDOR SEDAN, $590 | FORDOR SEDAN, $685 | COUPE, $525 | (All prices f. o. b. Detroit) |

Ford
CLOSED CARS

Adverts for the Ford Motor Company tell us who they were trying to sell their cars to. This one is from 1924. It is aimed at women drivers.

Inventions

Some of Henry's inventions have survived for us to look at now. This is Henry Ford's first car. It was called the Quadricycle because it ran on four bicycle wheels.

This is a Ford Tri-Motor aeroplane. It was the first all metal aeroplane with more than one **engine**. It had three engines. It carried passengers and mail.

The Henry Ford Museum

Henry Ford set up his own museum in Dearborn. He made copies of famous buildings, including the Wright Brothers' cycle shop (shown here) where they **designed** the first aeroplane.

The Henry Ford Museum contains many papers, photos and **artefacts** from Henry's life. This photo shows Henry hitting a car made from a type of plastic, to show how strong it was!

Glossary

This glossary explains difficult words and helps you to say words which may be hard to say.

artefact thing which people make and use. You say *art-ee-fact*.

assembly line system where workers line up along a conveyor belt. Each person does one small job to make something, like a car.

carriage vehicle to travel in, with wheels, pulled by horses

design to work out how to build a new invention

engine machine that makes the power to push something along. You say *en-jin*.

engineer person who makes and works with machines that are driven by engines

factory place where lots of people work making one thing, like cars. They use machines to do some of the work.

illuminating when you illuminate something, you light it up

mass produced things are mass produced when lots of them are made all the same. They are the same shape and size and are made from the same materials.

popular something a lot of people like

radio sending sounds through the air. People at the airport could talk to the people flying the aeroplane.

steam engine engine run by steam power. The steam is made by burning coal or wood.

Index

LIVES AND TIMES

- ● Who was Henry Ford?
- ● Why is he famous?
- ● How do we know about him?

This innovative series introduces young readers to the lives of famous men and women. Each beautifully illustrated life story is supported by primary source material, encouraging children to discover how we find out about past and recent history.

Each book contains:
- ● an accessible story and analysis of the evidence
- ● written and pictorial primary source material
- ● a glossary, pronunciation guide and index.

Titles in the series include:

Janet and Allan Ahlberg	0 431 02318 2	Alexander Graham Bell	0 431 02329 8
Bach	0 431 02313 1	Thomas Edison	0 431 02328 X
Beethoven	0 431 02314 X	Henry Ford	0 431 02330 1
Mozart	0 431 02316 6	Anne Frank	0 431 02327 1
Prokofiev	0 431 02315 8	Florence Nightingale	0 431 02516 9
Dr. Seuss	0 431 02317 4	Pack of 5	0 431 02331 X
Pack of 6	0 431 02319 0		

For other titles in the series see our website at www.heinemann.co.uk

ISBN 0-431-02330-1

9 780431 023304

Heinemann LIBRARY

The Life and Work of...

Mary Cassatt

Heinemann
firSt
Library